TREES

OF LODI GARDEN

Lodi Garden has something like 110 species of trees, give or take a few. It's hard to be absolutely precise about the number because there is room for arguing about whether or not a particular species qualifies as a tree. It's also true that the Garden occasionally loses solitary representatives of a species - we lost a beautiful young baobab tree *(Adansonia digitata)* in 1998 and more recently, in 2004, a mature West Indian elm *(Guazuma ulmifolia).* (That's one reason we have occasional blanks in our numbered list.) On the other hand, new species get planted from time to time, so the number of tree species does not hold steady.

These pages are an introduction to Lodi Garden's tree flora. Enjoy it, for there's lots to explore and appreciate. The Tree Map aims at being exhaustive, though you may find it a little hard sometimes, to pinpoint an individual in a dense stand. The Map is marked with a grid, and the Tree List has a grid reference for each tree, so that you can locate at least one specimen of any species that interests you.

In the Tree List, 7 of the best known trees have been labelled with a letter of the alphabet. The rest are numbered, the palms prefixed by the letter 'P'. The following format is used in the List:

TREE NO. COMMON NAME MAP GRID REF
Botanical Name (+ *recent, discarded name, if relevant)*
OTHER COMMON NAMES (in English and Hindi)
Brief description of the tree.

N NEEM C7

Azadirachta indica

MARGOSA

The familiar neem ('nature's pharmacy') is evergreen in moist areas, but goes bare briefly in March in Delhi. Lovely in new leaf. It has small, white, honey-scented flowers in April.

A AMALTAAS B7

Cassia fistula

INDIAN LABURNUM alaash; kirwara

Delhi's most spectacular native flowering tree, with long, pendant clusters of bright yellow flowers in May. The fruit are long cylindrical pipes, black when ripe.

G GULMOHUR E5

Delonix regia

FLAMETREE; FLAMBOYANT

A spectacular ornamental tree from Madagascar with light, feathery foliage and bright scarlet blossoms in April-May. Some people call it the most beautiful flowering tree of all.

P PEEPAL E5

Ficus religiosa

BO TREE; SACRED FIG

A large, deciduous 'strangler-fig', found in dry forests throughout India. Its long-tipped glossy leaves on long leaf stalks clatter noisily in the slightest breeze.

A AMALTAAS

M MAULSHREE G1

Mimusops elengi

INDIAN MEDLAR; BULLETWOOD bakul

A middle-sized, low-branching, evergreen tree with a dense, glossy crown. It bears fragrant, white, star-shaped flowers early in the rains.

K KABULI KEEKAR H1

Prosopis juliflora

MESQUITE; SOUTHWEST THORN vilaiti keekar

A pesky, invasive tree from South America with a crooked trunk, feathery crown and tiny flowers clustered on cylindrical spikes. It has run wild throughout Delhi.

J JAAMUN E3

Syzigium cumini

JAVA/BLACK PLUM phalinda

A handsome, near-evergreen tree with shining leaves and edible juicy berries, planted on avenues in New Delhi. Found wild especially near streams in dry forests throughout India.

1 EARPOD WATTLE G1

Acacia auriculiformis

DARWIN/NORTHERN BLACK WATTLE

A hardy acacia from Australia and New Guinea with leaf stalks modified into 'phyllodes' (that look deceptively like leaves) and bright yellow flowers in spikes after the rains.

2 RONJH G3

Acacia leucophloea

WHITE-BARKED ACACIA safed keekar

A thorny acacia with feathery foliage, an important part of Delhi's native flora. It bears tiny, creamy flowers clustered in spherical pom-poms at branch extremities late in the rains.

3 BUSHMAN'S POISON E2

Acokanthera spectabilis

WINTERSWEET; POISON ARROW PLANT

An evergreen shrub or modest tree from southern Africa, with clusters of intensely fragrant, white flowers in February. The milky juice is poisonous.

4 BAEL E7

Aegle marmelos

GOLDEN APPLE; BENGAL QUINCE beel; bila

A sacred tree with long spines and compound leaves with 3 leaflets. The fruit are large and woody with an orange pulp and have well-known medicinal properties.

5 KAURI PINE G3

Agathis robusta

QUEENSLAND KAURI

A flat-leaved conifer towering 16 storeys high in its native forests in Northern Australia. It remains stunted in Delhi's climate and does not flower or fruit here, but is still handsome.

6 KRISHNA SIRIS H2

Albizia amara

BITTER ALBIZIA

A deciduous, feathery-leaved tree easily mistaken for an acacia except that it lacks spines. Native to dry forests in central and southern India.

7 SIRIS D4

Albizia lebbeck

KOKO; EAST INDIAN WALNUT kali siris; sirin

A common, deciduous tree on Delhi's streets, with fragrant, yellow-green, tassel-like flowers and flat, straw-coloured pods that rattle noisily in the breeze. Native to dry forests in India.

8 DOON SIRIS D4

Albizia procera

WHITE SIRIS safed siris; karra

A slender, deciduous tree with a spare, feathery crown and distinctive creamy-yellow bark, native to marshy places in the sub-Himalayan tract.

9 BATINO C/D3

Alstonia macrophylla

HARD ALSTONIA

A slim, leggy tree from the Malay peninsula, unmistakably related to the satpatia but with longer, thinner and more pointy leaves. It has small, white flowers.

10 SATPATIA D4

Alstonia scholaris

DEVIL'S TREE; DITABARK saptaparni

A large, evergreen tree from the sub-Himalayan tract with milky sap and whorled leaves. It bears fragrant white flowers in October. Much planted on Delhi's avenues.

11 ULLOO H1

Ailanthus excelsa

TREE OF HEAVEN maharukh; mahaneem; ardu

A large tree with a great domed crown and coarsely toothed leaflets like a giant version of the neem's, smelling of peanuts when crushed.

12 CHAKWA E4

Anogeissus acuminata

AXLEWOOD; BUTTON TREE

A large, graceful tree from Myanmar with yellowish, mottled bark and small, silky leaves, especially when young. It bears tiny yellowish flowers in spherical clusters. Rare in Delhi.

13 BADHAL B5/6

Artocarpus lacucha

MONKEY JACK; LAKOOCH

A middle-sized, deciduous tree with densely woolly leaves (especially below) from the sub-Himalayan tract. Once cultivated for its fruit in Sabzi Mandi but now very rare in the city.

14 WILD LIME D5

Atalantia monophylla

INDIAN ATALANTIA jangli nimbu

A large bush or small, thorny tree with an unmistakably fluted stem, native to eastern and southern India. It flowers profusely but does not seem to set fruit in Delhi.

15 RED BARRINGTONIA A7

Barringtonia acutangula

FRESHWATER MANGROVE neora

A middle-sized tree that likes moist places, very widely distributed across Asia. It bears small scarlet flowers in long, pendulous clusters in August.

16 HONG KONG ORCHID TREE D5

Bauhinia x blakeana

RED-FLOWERED BAUHINIA

A natural hybrid first discovered in Canton (Southern China), widely cultivated for its splendid, orchid-like blossoms. It does not set fruit.

17 PURPLE BAUHINIA F5

Bauhinia purpurea

BUTTERFLY/GERANIUM TREE kaniaar; khairwaal

A smallish tree with delicate purple blossoms in October and characteristic camel's hoof-shaped leaves. Widely distributed, but not native to Delhi.

18 JHINJHERI D5

Bauhinia racemosa

BURMESE SILK ORCHID ashta; maula

A small, crooked tree with a beautiful, dense, spreading crown and inconspicuous, small white flowers. Native to the Ridge in Delhi but not very common.

19 KACHNAAR F5

Bauhinia variegata

MOUNTAIN EBONY; BUDDHIST BAUHINIA

A smallish tree from dry, deciduous forests in India (and further east), with beautiful flowers (in March) in shades of white and purple, and camel's hoof-shaped leaves.

20 SEMAL D7

Bombax ceiba

SILK COTTON; INDIAN KAPOK shembal

A lofty tree from grasslands in the terai with waxy blossoms, usually red but often yellow or coral-orange. Its seeds nestle in dense silky floss, used for stuffing pillows and mattresses.

21 BROADLEAVED BOTTLETREE C5/6

Brachychiton australis

BROADLEAVED KURRAJONG

An Australian tree belonging to the curious genus of 'bottletrees'. It has lobed maple-like leaves and small white flowers in March. Very rare in Delhi.

18 JHINJHERI

22 DESERT KURRAJONG E6

Brachychiton gregorii

An unusual tree from the arid Australian outback with greenish bark and long, narrow leaves that sometimes have 3-5 lobes. Like the other *Brachychiton*, it is very rare in Delhi.

23 PALAASH G1

Butea monosperma

FLAME OF THE FOREST; BENGAL KINO dhaak; tesu

A small crooked tree always with 3 large, leathery leaflets in its compound leaves and fiery bright orange blossoms in March-April. Wild on the Ridge.

24 CRIMSON BOTTLEBRUSH B6

Callistemon viminalis

WEEPING BOTTLEBRUSH

A small to middle-sized tree from NE Australia with slender drooping branches, narrow hairy leaves and bright scarlet flower-spikes shaped like bottlebrushes.

25 PINK MOHUR F5

Cassia javanica var. *indochinensis (=Cassia nodosa)*

PINK CASSIA; APPLEBLOSSOM SHOWER

A middle-sized, deciduous tree with a spreading crown. One of the prettiest of the pink cassias, flowering profusely. Native to SE Asia.

26 *Adansonia digitata* (baobab). Died 1998. RIP

27 CASUARINA B6

Casuarina equisetifolia

WHISTLING/AUSTRALIAN PINE; SHE-OAK jangli saru

A tall, graceful tree with drooping branchlets and scale-like leaves. Not really an oak or pine. Male and female trees are separate. Native to sandy beaches in tropical Asia and Australia.

28 KAPOK TREE E/F4/5

Ceiba pentandra

WHITE SILK COTTON safed semal

A towering Amazonian tree with a greenish trunk, obviously related to the semal but lacking its showy flowers. It is the source of 'true' kapok used in life jackets.

29 FLOSS-SILK TREE E6

Ceiba speciosa (=*Chorisia speciosa*)

MEXICAN SILK COTTON; CHORISIA

The most conspicuous flowering tree in Delhi after the rains. It has showy 5-petalled pink flowers when the tree is leafless and a distinctive green trunk when young.

30 KHIRK D3

Celtis tetrandra

EASTERN NETTLE TREE kharak; adona

A handsome, deciduous tree from lower Himalayan slopes, common in hedgerows in Lutyens' Delhi but no longer planted in the city. Very beautiful in new leaf in March.

31 CHIKRASSY E6

Chukrasia tabularis

CHITTAGONG WOOD; INDIAN REDWOOD chikrassi

A large tree from moist forests in India with an ample, spreading crown. Related to the neem. Newest leaflets are tinged red. It flowers erratically in Delhi.

32 COLVILLE'S GLORY B7

Colvillea racemosa

GLORY COLVILLEA

A slight, deciduous tree from Madagascar, easily mistaken at first glance for a gulmohur. Coppery patches on its bark and splendid orange blossoms (in July) are distinctive.

33 LASODA D6

Cordia dichotoma

CLAMMY/INDIAN CHERRY bhokar; gondi

A deciduous tree from Indian moist and dry forests with oval, coarsely toothed leaves and fruit like pale cherries. Possibly native to Delhi.

34 LEMON-SCENTED GUM E6

Corymbia citriodora (=Eucalyptus citriodora)

safeda

A slender gum-tree with a smooth pale grey trunk and open crown. Its urn-shaped gumnuts and lemon-scented leaves are useful in identification. This is one of the Eucalypts that has been placed in the new genus *Corymbia*.

35 BARNA E6/7

Crataeva adansonii subsp. *odora*

GARLIC PEAR; SACRED BARNA bilasi

A crooked native tree, leafless for a long period but breathtakingly beautiful in full flower (in early April). It has 3 leaflets in its compound leaf.

36 SHISHAM D2

Dalbergia sissoo

INDIAN ROSEWOOD sissoo; taali

A large, often crooked tree from alluvial riverbanks in the sub-Himalayan tract. Beautiful in new leaf in late March. The small white flowers are inconspicuous. Cultivated and highly valued for its heavy, hard timber, beautifully streaked and used for quality furniture.

37 BISTENDU

37 BISTENDU E1

Diospyros cordifolia

bassendu; passendu

A smallish native Delhi tree with beautiful new foliage in April. Male and female trees are separate. The round, yellow fruit is the size of a ping-pong ball.

38 PUTRANJIVA E5/6

Drypetes roxburghii (=Putranjiva roxburghii)

WILD OLIVE; CHILD-LIFE TREE putranjia

An evergreen tree from moist forests in India with graceful, drooping, glossy foliage. The tiny flowers are inconspicuous and male and female trees are separate. The seeds are strung together as rosaries.

39 CHAMROR D2

Ehretia laevis

desi paapdi; datranga

A hardy native tree usually with a gnarled, knobbly, pale trunk. Most conspicuous when it bears clusters of white, star-shaped flowers very early in spring.

40 EARPOD TREE D5

Enterolobium contortisiliquum
(=Enterolobium timbouva)

ELEPHANT EAR; MONKEYSOAP

A relative of the siris from tropical S America, with a massive, deeply fissured trunk and pretty foliage. It bears small, woolly, cream-coloured flowers in March.

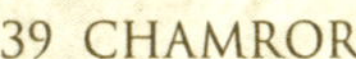

39 CHAMROR

41 INDIAN CORAL TREE E2

Erythrina variegata var. *orientalis*

TIGER'S CLAW TREE mandara; tota

A spiny, ornamental tree with brilliant scarlet blossoms and compound leaves with 3 large leaflets. Widely distributed in coastal areas throughout tropical Asia.

42 RIVER RED GUM F4

Eucalyptus camaldulensis var. *obtusa*

MURRAY RED GUM safeda

Probably the best-loved of all Australian eucalypts with its creamy, mottled bark and heavy, twisting branches. Together with the variety listed below (number 43), very widely planted around the world.

43 RIVER RED GUM F4

Eucalyptus camaldulensis var. *camaldulensis*

MURRAY RED GUM safeda

Distinguished from number 42 (above) by a stocking of darker bark and small, pointy flower buds. Being close together, it is easy to spot the differences between these two varieties of the same species.

44 FOREST RED GUM F4

Eucalyptus tereticornis

MYSORE GUM; EUCALYPTUS HYBRID safeda

The most common species of eucalyptus in Delhi, with a thin crown and upswept branches. The buds wear a long, conical 'pixie-cap'. A variable species but not a hybrid.

45 KATSAAGON E1

Fernandoa adenophyllum

(=Haplophragma adenophyllum)

marodphali

A tall, quick-growing, somewhat untidy tree from NE India. It bears pale yellow bell-shaped flowers in the rains, and has long, curly, cylindrical pods.

46 BARGAD D5/6

Ficus benghalensis

BANYAN TREE badh; bor

A familiar 'strangler-fig' that often begins life on another tree, then goes on to form a gigantic canopy with its endless prop-roots. It bears large red figs in pairs.

47 MAKKHAN KATORA E4

Ficus benghalensis var. *krishnae*

KRISHNA'S BUTTERCUP krishna badh

A small-sized variety of the Bargad with curious leaves whose lower edge is turned up into a "pocket". Grown as a curiosity and considered sacred to Lord Krishna.

48 WEEPING FIG E4

Ficus benjamina var. *comosa*

JAVA FIG/WILLOW;WEEPING LAUREL kabra

A large fig tree with a dense crown of glossy, drooping foliage. It has (literally) hundreds of cultivars, many of which were created as indoor tub-plants.

49 INDIA RUBBER TREE D4

Ficus elastica

RUBBER TREE; ASSAM RUBBER

A strangler-fig that reaches 50 m in north-east India but is stunted in Delhi. Once grown for its latex which yielded 'India rubber', now merely a glossy-leaved ornamental fig-tree.

50 LAUREL FIG G4

Ficus microcarpa (=Ficus retusa)

INDIAN LAUREL; CHINESE BANYAN usba; chilkhan

A large evergreen fig tree with glossy, blunt-tipped leaves that grows to a massive size. It usually has dense aerial roots tightly wrapped around the top of its trunk.

51 PILKHAN E4

Ficus virens (=Ficus infectoria)

GREY/SPOTTED FIG paakad; ram anjeer

A deciduous fig-tree that develops a massive, top-heavy shady crown. Its white figs are spotted with red and its aerial roots do not reach the ground. Possibly native to Delhi.

52 GOOLAR D4

Ficus racemosa (=Ficus glomerata)

CLUSTER FIG umar; trimbal

A water-loving, deciduous, native fig-tree. The only species in Delhi whose figs grow in branching clusters from the trunk and main branches.

53 JADI F4

Ficus amplissima (=Ficus tsiela)

pimpri

A deciduous 'strangler-fig' easily mistaken for the pilkhan. You can tell them apart by its yellowish trunk and its ripe figs which are stalkless and purple when ripe. Not native to Delhi.

51 PILKHAN

54 SILKY OAK D4

Grevillea robusta

SILVER OAK; RIVER OAK

A tall, slender Australian tree. Its bright orange brush-like blossoms are unusual and very beautiful. It is, of course, not really an oak at all.

55 *Guazuma ulmifolia*. Died 2004. RIP

56 KANJU E1

Holoptelea integrifolia

INDIAN ELM paapdi; chudail-paapdi

Delhi's tallest native tree. Its trunk is often buttressed and though its tiny flowers are inconspicuous, the masses of flat papery fruits (in April) are distinctive.

57 JACARANDA F1

Jacaranda mimosaefolia

BRAZILIAN ROSEWOOD neeli gulmohur

A familiar South American tree with a thin, open crown. Chiefly grown for its splendid blue, trumpet-flowers that appear when the tree is leafless.

58 PHYSIC NUT A6

Jatropha curcas

PURGING/BARBADOS NUT jangli arand

A soft-wooded, deciduous shrub or small tree from tropical America with milky juice and lobed leaves. Its seeds are a violent purgative.

59 CHINESE JUNIPER D3

Juniperus chinensis

A small, coniferous tree with a narrow conical form. If you look carefully, you can see that it always bears both adult scale-leaves and juvenile needle-leaves on the same plant.

60 JARUL A7

Lagerstroemia speciosa (=*Lagerstroemia flos-reginae*)

QUEEN'S FLOWER; PRIDE OF INDIA motabandara

One of Delhi's most beautiful flowering trees, with showy mauve, pink or lilac flowers produced in May-June. Native to moist forests in NE and S India.

61 SUBABOOL G4

Leucaena leucocephala

WHITE POPINAC; HORSE TAMARIND

A small, unarmed mimosa from South America that was introduced to India as a 'miracle tree' for green manure and animal fodder. It has not been an unqualified success and has become weedy and invasive.

62 SOUTHERN MAGNOLIA F5

Magnolia grandiflora

BULL BAY; LOBLOLLY himchampa

A beautiful, evergreen flowering tree from the southern USA. It has thick, leathery leaves and fragrant pure white blossoms in April-May. Stunted in Delhi's climate.

63 AAM C7

Mangifera indica

MANGO amb

The familiar mango can grow to an immense size in the right conditions, but is stunted and unhappy in Delhi. It likes a lot of moisture and deep soil.

64 KHIRNI C5

Manilkara hexandra

CEYLON IRONWOOD khinni; rayan

A long-lived, evergreen tree related to the chikoo. Possibly one of Delhi's oldest cultivated trees but not native to this region.

65 MOULMEIN ROSEWOOD E4

Millettia peguensis (=*Millettia ovalifolia*)

JEWELS ON A STRING

Native to dry forests in Myanmar and Thailand, this pretty tree is grown for its splendid mauve flowers produced en masse early in April.

66 KAIM E5

Mitragyna parviflora

kallam; kadamb

A native Delhi tree that grows wild in gravelly beds of seasonal streams. It has beautiful small flowers arranged in tight spheres. This is the 'kadamb' associated with Brindavan.

67 TOOT G4

Morus alba

WHITE/CHINESE MULBERRY toont; shahtoot

This is the silkworm mulberry, originally from China but cultivated in India for thousands of years. It can now be called a naturalized native.

68 KAAMINI D5

Murraya paniculata

ORANGE JESSAMINE; MOCK ORANGE marchula

Delhi's favourite hedge-plant. In dry forests, it forms a small, crooked tree. The white flowers, produced in repeated flushes, are deliciously fragrant.

69 KADAMB F4

Neolamarckia cadamba (=*Anthocephalus cadamba*)

CADAMBA

A slim, tall, fast-growing tree native to moist forests in NE India, with beautiful foliage and flowers arranged in spherical clusters. Mistakenly associated with Brindavan. (See no. 66)

70 HARSHINGAAR H3

Nyctanthes arbor-tristis

NIGHT-BLOOMING JASMINE; TREE OF SORROW

A small tree from dry, deciduous jungles with rough leaves but heavenly night-blooming flowers that fall to the ground each morning after the rainy season.

71 BIRD'S EYE BUSH C6

Ochna obtusata

GOLDEN CHAMPAK ramdhan champa

A small tree native to eastern India, with beautiful, bright yellow flowers that emerge along with its new leaves in April-May.

72 RUSTY SHIELD BEARER F2

Peltophorum pterocarpum

(=Peltophorum ferrugineanum)

COPPERPOD; YELLOW FLAME peeli gulmohur

A large tree from coastal E Asia and the Andamans with a spreading crown. Its crinkly yellow crepe-like flowers are outstandingly beautiful and faintly fragrant.

73 CHINESE ARBOR-VITAE D2

Platycladus orientalis (=Thuja orientalis)

ORIENTAL THUJA morpankhi

A densely branched conifer branching low down, native to W China and Korea, cultivated for ornament in hundreds of named cultivars.

74 SINGAPORE PLUMERIA D2

Plumeria obtusa

WHITE/CUBAN FRANGIPANI khair champa

A nearly evergreen tree with milky latex from tropical America, with fragrant clusters of large white flowers. There are many different varieties and hybrids.

75 TEMPLE TREE G4

Plumeria rubra

MEXICAN FRANGIPANI champa

Like the Singapore plumeria (no. 74), this too is originally from tropical America and has spawned many cultivars. It is distinguished by its pointy leaves, which are deciduous.

76 CHIR PINE D1

Pinus roxburgii

LONGLEAVED/KUMAON PINE cheed

One of the few pine-trees to grow in Delhi, from hot, dry slopes in the lower Himalaya. Distinguished by having 3 needles in each cluster.

77 ASHOK E7

Polyalthia longifolia

MAST TREE debdaru; ashupaal

A glossy-leaved, evergreen tree widely cultivated in India for its slim, cypress-like shape. Native to monsoon forests in Sri Lanka. Its pale greenish flowers are not conspicuous.

78 KARANJ F1

Pongamia pinnata (=Pongamia glabra)

INDIAN BEECH paapdi; sukhchain

A squat-trunked spreading tree growing wild along streams in dry forests. It is widely cultivated in cities at least partly because saplings are not browsed by goats!

79 COTTONWOOD F6

Populus deltoides

EASTERN COTTONWOOD bagnoo

Native to deserts in Southeastern USA and known to be the fastest growing tree on the North American continent. Cultivated in northern India for its fast-growing sapling poles.

80 JHAND G2

Prosopis cinerarea

jaat; saangri; khejdi

A hardy Delhi native with feathery foliage, adapted to harsh, arid conditions. It produces tiny yellow flowers in long spikes in spring. The bark is rough and deeply fissured.

81 KANAKCHAMPA E3

Pterospermum acerifolium

MAPLE-LEAVED BAYUR muchkand

A large, nearly evergreen tree from sub-Himalayan tracts with large, dark, lobed leaves and fragrant, pure white flowers in early spring.

82 NARIKEL B7

Pterygota alata

BUDDHA'S COCONUT

Lodi Gardens' tallest tree, a lone, large-leaved specimen from rainforests in NE and S India. Once the favoured roost of vultures (before vultures had been killed off by Diclofenac).

83 SAND PEAR F1

Pyrus pyrifolia (=Pyrus sinensis)

JAPANESE/ASIAN PEAR naakh

A smallish, pretty tree with pure white flowers and small, hard pears. From China and Japan, where it has been cultivated for at least 3,000 years.

80 JHAND

84. PHILIPPINE TUNG TREE F4

Reutealis trisperma (=Aleurites trisperma)

SOFT LUMBANG

A smallish tree from SE Asia with pretty white flowers and very long-stalked, heart-shaped leaves. An uncommon tree in Delhi.

85. SITA-ASHOK H3

Saraca asoca

SORROWLESS TREE ashok

Some people call this tree from NE India our most beautiful tree for its exquisite, bright red flowers. It struggles in Delhi's dry climate and produces no fruit here.

86 PEELU D3

Salvadora persica

MUSTARD/TOOTHBRUSH TREE jaal

A desert tree of great character with a wonderful gnarled, twisted trunk and small, pink fruit with a peppery tang. Native to Delhi, but becoming rare.

87 KOSAM F1

Schleichera oleosa

LAC TREE; CEYLON OAK kusum; kasma

A large forest tree with a broad, shady crown. The flowers are inconspicuous but its new leaves are spectacular in various shades of deep red and pink.

86 PEELU

88 KASSOD D6

Senna siamea (=*Cassia siamea*)

SIAMESE SENNA; IRONWOOD

A commonly cultivated tree from SE Asia with large clusters of pale yellow flowers (twice a year) produced at the ends of its branches.

89 GLAUCOUS CASSIA B7

Senna surattensis (=*Cassia surattensis*)

KALAMONA; SCRAMBLED EGGS

A tall shrub or modest tree with splendid, bright yellow flowers after the rains. Its precise origins are uncertain – probably SE Asia.

90 *Senna spectabilis*. Died 2004. RIP

91 CARIBBEAN TRUMPET TREE F4

Tabebuia aurea (=*Tabebuia argentea*)

PARAGUAYAN/SILVER TRUMPET TREE

A small, crooked tree from dry forests in S America with thick corky bark and brilliant yellow trumpet-flowers. Introduced into Delhi in the 1970s.

92 PINK TRUMPET TREE F3

Tabebuia impetiginosa

PALMER TRUMPET TREE

This is another S American tabebuia with beautiful trumpet-flowers, only these ones are pink. It is often mistakenly called '*Tabebuia rosea*'.

93 MONTEZUMA CYPRESS D3

Taxodium mucronatum

BALD CYPRESS; MEXICAN SWAMP CYPRESS

A slender-leaved tree from the Sonoran desert in Mexico, where it grows to immense sizes. One of the few conifers to shed its leaves.

94 ROHEDA

94 ROHEDA G1

Tecomella undulata

WAVY-LEAVED TECOMELLA lahura; luaar

A small, crooked, native tree from arid parts of NW India. It produces bright orange blossoms in March. The tree is believed to cure skin diseases and the clothes of young children are often hung on the tree in the hope that the tree will cure the children of skin infections.

95 TEAK TREE C3

Tectona grandis saagwaan

A tall, rough-leaved tree from S Indian forests that provides the much-prized teak wood. Not very common in Delhi.

96 ARJUN C3

Terminalia arjuna arjuna

A very large tree that grows naturally along riverbanks in Indian dry forests. Mostly cultivated in Delhi as an avenue tree. Its flowers are not conspicuous but the winged fruit are distinctive.

96 ARJUN

97 YELLOW OLEANDER C/D5

Thevetia peruviana

BE-STILL TREE; LUCKY NUT peeli kaner

A small, poisonous, evergreen tree from Mexico and the West Indies, with narrow shiny leaves and milky latex. Its bright yellow trumpet-flowers last for many months.

98 DOODHI D/E6

Wrightia tinctoria

PALA INDIGO; DYER'S OLEANDER kaaru

Native to dry forests throughout India, doodhi produces white, fragrant flowers in great profusion at the hottest time of the year. Also found wild on the Ridge.

PALMS

P1 JAGGERY PALM C5

Caryota urens

FISHTAIL/TODDY/WINE PALM mari; bankhajur

The only palm in Delhi with twice-divided compound leaves. The ends of its leaflets look like they've been chewed off. It bears flowers and fruit in large, pendulous 'pony-tails'.

P2 GOLDEN CANE PALM C4

Dypsis lutescens (=Chrysalidocarpus lutescens)

ARECA PALM

A graceful palm from Madagascar, widely cultivated for its slender, arching leaves. It usually grows in clumps and is also taken indoors as a tub-specimen. (The name 'areca palm' is misleading and should not be confused with the areca-nut or supari palm).

P3 CHINESE FAN PALM C5

Livistona chinensis

FOUNTAIN PALM

Probably Delhi's most common ornamental palm. It has large fan-shaped leaves with a characteristic droop to the splayed ends of its leaflets. It flowers in March.

P4 FOOTSTOOL PALM C5

Livistona rotundifolia

ROUNDLEAF/ANAHAW PALM

Similar to the Chinese fan palm, but lacking the drooping leaflets. Instead, its leaves are nearly circular in outline and the long leaf stalks are much more spiny.

P5 CALIFORNIAN FAN PALM C4

Washingtonia filifera

DESERT FAN/PETTICOAT PALM

The tallest palms in Lodi Garden, with huge fan-shaped leaves that tend to hang down in an untidy 'petticoat' when they die. Native to southern California, widely cultivated for ornament.

P6 WILD DATE PALM H1

Phoenix sylvestris

SUGAR DATE/SILVER DATE PALM khajuri; salma

This is the feather-leaved palm that you see depicted in ancient prints of Delhi's monuments. It grows self-sown in moist places and is widely distributed across the Indian subcontinent.

P7 CUBAN ROYAL PALM B7

Roystonia regia

BOTTLE PALM; MOUNTAIN GLORY

The regular cement-coloured trunks of these Caribbean feather-leaved palms are something of a cliché around historical monuments. Architects love them for their 'formal' effect.

P8 CABBAGE PALM C5

Sabal palmetto

PALMETTO/CAROLINA PALM

A distinctive palm with arching leaf stalks prolonged through to the ends of its large fan-leaves. The trunk is usually adorned with 'boots', the criss-cross remains of fallen leaf stalks. Beautiful when it flowers in April-May. From SE USA.

P9 SAVANNAH PALM C5

Sabal mauritiiformis

BAY PALMETTO

A distinctive palm with huge, floppy leaves deeply divided to their bases, tending to look somewhat ragged. The trunk is ringed and like the cabbage palm (above) usually retains the 'boots' of old leaves.

INDEX

FOR LODI GARDEN TREES

NOTES

NOTES

NOTES

AN INTRODUCTION TO LODI GARDEN

The Lodi Garden was designed in 1936 as a setting for a group of fine, five-hundred-year old buildings that were particularly worthy of preservation. At that time South Delhi was nothing like it is now. During the nineteenth century the landscape around Delhi was compared with the surroundings of Rome, empty but with many impressive remains of former empires. In 1931, when Lutyen's New Delhi was nearing completion, the whole area of South Delhi had changed little and was described as 'a flat country, brown, scrubby, and broken', studded with ruins. In the 1930s the Lodi Tombs stood in the village of Khairpur, on the outskirts of New Delhi. In 1936 the villagers were moved from Khairpur and the garden was laid out with native and exotic trees and plants around the monuments. It was at first called Lady Willingdon Park, after the wife of the then British Viceroy. After Independence, it was named more appropriately as Lodi Garden and was re-landscaped in 1968. Today the Lodi and Sayyid tombs and their garden setting is a place for picnickers, joggers and those looking for a quiet place amidst the bustle of Delhi. The historic Lodi Garden is very special, and requires our continued care and protection.

HISTORICAL BACKGROUND

Since the 12th century Delhi was the capital of a series of Afghan and Turk rulers. The Sayyids established their small Sultanate in the 15th century. Muhammed Shah, who ruled Delhi between 1434-44, was the third Sayyid ruler. His son Alauddin Alam Shah probably built his father's tomb, the oldest tomb in the Gardens.

The Lodi dynasty (1451-1526) originated from an Afghan tribe that had been long settled in India. They seized power from the Sayyids and re-established the importance of the Delhi Sultanate. They ruled over an area stretching from the banks of the Indus, over Punjab and the Ganga Yamuna doab to the borders of Bengal, and southwards into central India.

Bahlol, the first Lodi king, seized the throne from the Sayyids. His son Sikandar, reigned for 28 years (1489 1517). Sikandar built his capital at Agra. A town named Sikandra, not far from Agra and now famous for the tomb of Emperor Akbar, is named after this great Lodi king.

Sikandar was succeeded by his son Ibrahim who was defeated at Panipat in 1526 by Babur. It was Babur who established the Mughal Empire in India.

THE DESIGN OF THE BUILDINGS

Islam brought many innovative ideas to India. In India, before the 12th century, builders created magnificent structures using a system of posts and beams in which the space between two pillars or walls was spanned with a single stone piece called a lintel. A system of corbelling using smaller blocks of stone, projecting one above the other, provided extra support for the lintel. No cement or binding material was used in this post and beam engineering principle. This meant that the doorways were narrow and large halls were crowded with many pillars.

The arch, originally invented by the Romans, was used throughout the Islamic world and brought to India in the 12th century. The builder could now span a greater distance between two pillars or walls by using smaller blocks of stone, balanced by a keystone to form an arch. This engineering principle transformed buildings and gave them a new design with huge open doorways and halls that were not cluttered with pillars and high ceilings.

When the arch was introduced into India, the Indian builder was at first hesitant to use it. With characteristic ingenuity, the architects of early Islamic buildings combined the two engineering traditions to create what we now call Indo Islamic architecture. In the Lodi monuments look out for such examples where an arch, belonging to the new system, is placed above pillars, ornate lintels and supporting brackets or corbels that were derived from an older tradition.

The *gumbad* or domed roof of the building was built using the principle of the arch. An interesting problem arose here. How could the architect support a circular roof on a square building? The problem was solved by converting the four walls of the building into a drum that had 8, then 16, then 32 and then 64 sides - almost a circle. The transformation and transition of the square to the circle was achieved by squinches and corbels.

What you see in the Lodi Garden is part of a tradition that was to influence architecture and building in the subcontinent for the next five hundred years.

In West and Central Asia buildings were embellished with ceramic tiles, plasterwork and painted decorations. Multicoloured tiles were used to adorn the domes and outer walls of the buildings. The tiles were glazed turquoise blue, midnight blue, leaf green, sunlight yellow and brick red, cut to size and assembled to create intricate patterns and geometric designs of interwoven squares, circles, and lines. Although tilework was seldom used lavishly in India, many buildings were enhanced by the addition of tiles, for instance on domes and parts of the façades. Look for the few remains of brightly coloured tiles on the buildings, and try to imagine the splendour of the past.

THE MOSQUE

The most important building for any community is the place of prayer. The *masjid* or mosque is a place for Muslims to pray. It consists of an open or covered space for communal prayer where the people face the direction of Mecca (in India, therefore, towards the west). The centre of the prayer wall is always marked by an ornate niche called the *mihrab*. There is sometimes a *mihrab* on the western wall of tomb chambers, though there is often a separate mosque as well.

SETTING FOR THE ROYAL TOMBS

Tombs were generally constructed outside the city, sometimes built by rulers and nobles in anticipation of their death. The Afghan tribal chiefs viewed a king not as the absolute authority but more as a comrade, the first among equals. The nobles of the Lodi court felt they too merited tombs; this explains the many large tombs constructed during the Lodi period in Delhi.

The site of such tombs was often chosen for its proximity to the burial place of a great person such as a holy man or a king. It was sometimes selected for its landscape value. We do not know why this area in particular was chosen for the tombs of Sayyid and Lodi rulers. These buildings were situated near a tributary of the Yamuna. During Lodi times, this tributary would have formed an integral part of the landscape. The construction of the bridge called Athpula (eight arches) is attributed to Nawab Bahadur, a nobleman at Emperor Akbar's court. The once deep *nala* (watercourse) has been sadly reduced to an ornamental lake that remains dry for some of the year.

THE TOMB

Throughout the Islamic world the dead are buried in graves with a tombstone or cenotaph over the vault in which the body lies. The belief is that after death the soul will be judged, and the good will go to paradise. Therefore, it was important to care for and respect tombs. The body was laid so that, if turned on its side, it faced Mecca, the direction of prayer. The grave was traditionally placed under 'the canopy of the sky'. Often, in the tomb-chambers of important people, the metaphor of the sky was converted into huge masonry domes or *gumbad*, and the ceilings were decorated with motifs of stars and other celestial bodies.

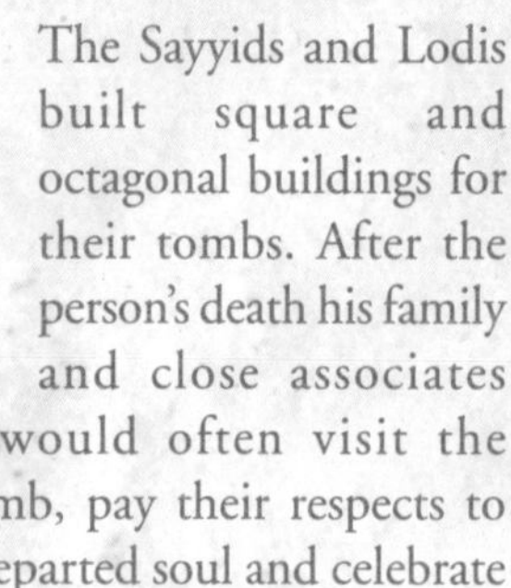

The Sayyids and Lodis built square and octagonal buildings for their tombs. After the person's death his family and close associates would often visit the tomb, pay their respects to the departed soul and celebrate anniversaries. The evolution of the square and octagonal tomb buildings in Islamic architecture led to the spectacular Mughal buildings: Humayun's tomb and Mumtaz Mahal's tomb, the Taj Mahal.

OTHER PLACES TO VISIT

Hauz Khas Madrasa

There are many other historic sites to visit in south Delhi, some of them set in beautiful gardens: the buildings at Firoz Shah Kotla and Hauz Khas are older than the Lodi tombs *(Hauz Khas Madrasa)*, while the Purana Qila, Humayun's Tomb and Safdarjang's Tomb are all more recent. Near the Qutb Minar is the Mehrauli Archaeological Park, where there are many ruined buildings from different periods in a semi-wild setting.

Humayun's Tomb

Ruined tomb or gateway in Archaeological Park, Mehrauli

If you want to see examples of the kind of architecture that came before the Lodi tombs you can visit sites like the Qutb Minar and Tughlakabad.

Ghiyasuddin Tughlak's tomb at Tughlakabad

Other fine examples of Lodi tombs can be seen in South Extension Part 1, Hauz Khas Deer Park and RKPuram, where there are several large tombs in each place. Apart from an octagonal tomb in Kotla Mubarakpur (where Muhammad Shah's father is buried), these are all square tombs. If you go to look at them you will notice the variation in size and ornamentation.

Bare Khan ka Gumbad, near Kotla Mubarakpur

Apart from the massive tombs built for Humayun and Safdarjang, there are a great many smaller tombs that were built during the Mughal period. These all demonstrate the change in architectural style following the arrival of the Mughal dynasty.

NB some of these sites charge entrance fees.

Atgah Khan's Tomb, Nizamuddin

Tomb in Sundar Bagh Nursery, near Humayun's Tomb

LODI GARDEN

A WALK THROUGH HISTORY

Welcome to the Lodi Garden, once called Bagh I-Jud, the royal burial ground for Sayyid and Lodi rulers of Delhi.

Use the map to visit the wonderful historical buildings and royal tombs in this garden. You can enter Lodi Garden from different gates.

The introduction to the monuments is in chronological sequence.

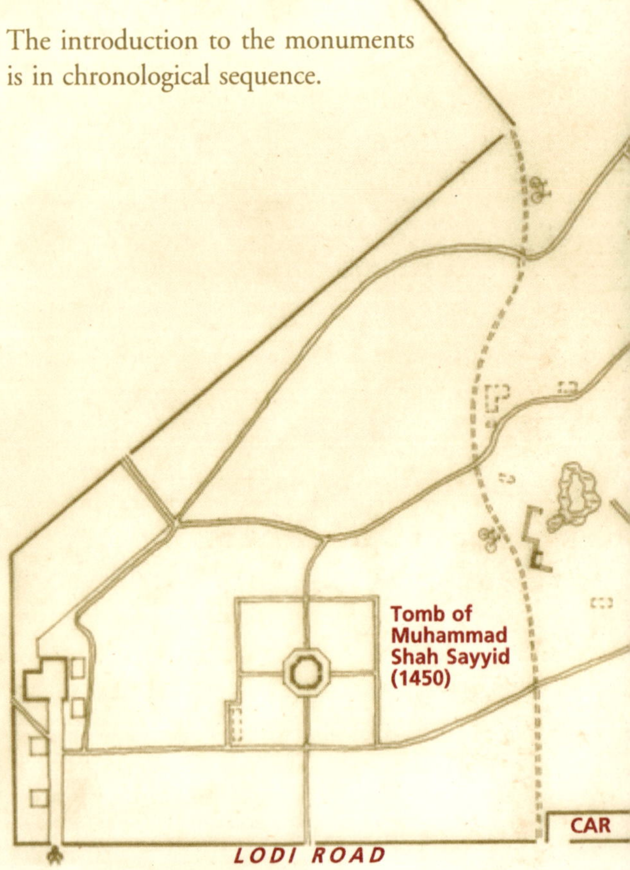

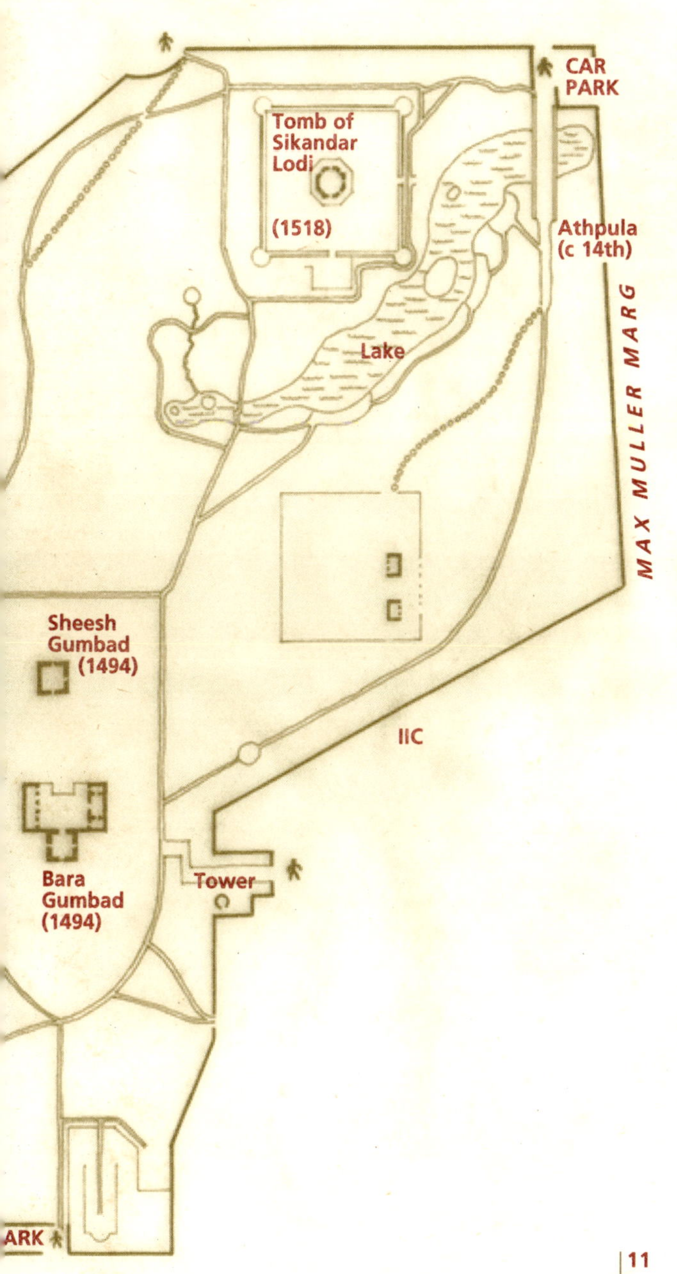
CAR
PARK
Tomb of
Sikandar
Lodi
(1518)
Athpula
(c 14th)
Lake
MAX MULLER MARG
Sheesh
Gumbad
(1494)
IIC
Bara
Gumbad
(1494)
Tower
ARK

TOMB OF MUHAMMAD SHAH SAYYID

This is the oldest tomb in the gardens. This handsome building stands on a platform. An arched verandah surrounds the central octagonal chamber, in the middle of which lies the cenotaph of Muhammad Shah, surrounded by several others. The dome of the building is large, gracefully proportioned, and raised on a drum. A cluster of small domed *chhatris* (pavilion or, literally, umbrella) surrounds the main dome. Such clusters of *chhatris*, like the sun with its orbit of planets, can also be seen in the tomb of Humayun in Delhi and the Taj Mahal in Agra.

The tomb is decorated, as was the tradition, with incised stucco plasterwork. While the plaster was wet it was carved with patterns. When dry the plaster was painted with many colours like a jewel box, to create a perfect resting place for the king.

BARA GUMBAD

The name literally means the building with a big (bara) dome (gumbad). Some scholars feel this was not a tomb because there is no sign of a grave and therefore it may have been a gateway. Adjoining the tomb on the west is a mosque, with a pavilion to the east. The group of buildings is raised on a high platform in the middle of which is a raised area that might have been a grave platform.

The Bara Gumbad is the largest structure and, seen from outside, would appear to have two storeys. However, when you enter you will see that it has a single chamber with a magnificent high ceiling. The decoration is minimal with the pale grey quartzite relieved by pink sandstone and grey-black highlights. The doorways are corbelled.

A mosque was placed on the west wall of the tomb platform. This mosque, though small, is remarkably beautiful. The mosque has five arched openings with spectacular stucco work of floral motifs and geometric designs. These arches lead into a rectangular prayer hall that has calligraphic inscriptions and decorated ceilings.

One of the inscriptions, dated 1494, says that a noble, Mughal Abu Amjad, erected the mosque during the reign of Sikander Lodi, who is described as 'the king of the inhabited fourth part of the globe'.

On the opposite side of the platform is a pavilion, probably used to accommodate pilgrims or attendants at the mosque. This pavilion creates a sense of balance and complements the mosque, while framing the Bara Gumbad.

SHEESH GUMBAD

This building is called the 'Sheesh Gumbad', or glass dome. The dome and parts of the façade were once completely covered with coloured glazed tiles. You can see remnants of its former elegance in the turquoise and cobalt-blue tile work on the facade.

The central tomb chamber has several graves, presumably of eminent people of Sikandar Lodi's time. This building does not have a separate mosque like Bara Gumbad; here there is a *mihrab* on the inner western wall.

TOWER/TURRET

It is not known what this building was. It may have been a corner turret of an enclosure, the walls of which have completely disappeared. In style it appears to date from a slightly earlier period than the other buildings in the garden.

TOMB OF SIKANDAR LODI

This is set in a square garden, enclosed within high walls that make it look like a little fortress. The idea of an enclosed tomb-garden appears first in Ghiyas ud din Tughlak's tomb near Tughlakabad, and there are grander later versions: Humayun's tomb, Taj Mahal, and Safdarjang's tomb. The tomb garden as it is maintained today, does not give us a clear sense of how it may have looked five hundred years ago. On the west side of the inner walls of Sikandar Lodi's tomb is a wall-mosque. On the south is a platform with another wall-mosque and small chattris decorated with tiles. This may have been an earlier tomb structure converted to form a grand entrance to the tomb.

The octagonal tomb's inner chamber is surrounded by a lovely verandah of arches with carved sandstone brackets.

Inside the tomb chamber are some well-preserved and beautifully-designed glazed tile decorations, and painted stucco-work.

ATHPULA

Athpula is a picturesque bridge to the east of Sikandar Lodi's tomb. *Ath* means eight and *pula* means bridge/piers. Sadly some of the arches now lie buried, so the name appears incorrect. This bridge is believed to have been built during Akbar's reign to span a tributary of the Yamuna, a part of the river system that drained the south Delhi area.

OTHER REMAINS

The area was clearly in use during the Mughal period and several remains of buildings and tombs can be seen in various parts of the garden. Look for the walled Mughal garden that contains two lovely pavilions.

NOTES

NOTES

NOTES

NOTES